WONDER & WRECKAGE

WONDER & WRECKAGE

New & Selected Poems, 1993 – 2023

By Collin Kelley

Poetry Atlanta Press

ALSO BY COLLIN KELLEY

Poetry
Better To Travel
HalfLife Crisis
Slow To Burn
After the Poison
Render
Midnight in a Perfect World

Novels
Conquering Venus
Remain In Light
Leaving Paris

Short Stories
Kiss Shot

Poetry Atlanta Press

Wonder & Wreckage: New & Selected Poems, 1993-2023
Copyright 2024 by Collin Kelley

Cover Design: Elizabeth Price Holmes
Author Photo: Collin Kelley, Self-Portrait

Poetry Atlanta Press
800 Peachtree St. NE
Suite 1503
Atlanta, GA 30308
www.facebook.com/poetryatlanta

ISBN: 979-8-218-40724-7

First Edition

For Terry Graves

CONTENTS

Entr'acte

3. Play it as it Lays

INTRODUCTION: THE DIRECTOR'S CUT

I've been a film and music fanatic since I was a child. From being awestruck by *Star Wars* and *Superman: The Movie*, to finding a deep resonance with the films of Wim Wenders (*Wings of Desire*), Krystof Kieslowski (*Three Colors trilogy*), Sally Potter (*Orlando*) and Derek Jarman (*Edward II*).

I have a distinct memory of being in the backseat of my parent's puke-green Ford LTD the first time I heard "Dreams" by Fleetwood Mac, Debbie Harry cooing over the disco beat of Blondie's "Heart of Glass" on the radio in my grandmother's kitchen, Kate Bush somersaulting across my late-night television screen singing "Wuthering Heights," and Peter Gabriel leading me to the poetry of Anne Sexton with "Mercy Street."

While most poets get their formal training by reading other poets and getting literature degrees, my first teachers were filmmakers and musicians.

So, it seemed appropriate that the framework of this new & selected collection should pay homage to those early loves and educators. I've always been intrigued by directors taking a finished film and adding to the story to present a "final" or "ultimate" version of the story they wanted to tell uninhibited by studio demands and clashes over artistic vision.

Ridley Scott finally arrived at his perfect vision of *Blade Runner* 30 years after its initial release. Adrian Lyne's original ending for *Fatal Attraction* – where Alex Forrest takes her own life and gains the upper hand over asshole Dan Gallagher – is the superior and haunting finale audiences deserved. Perhaps the greatest example is Wenders' *Until the End of the World*, which he was forced to cut to two hours, but had secretly held on to the five-hour version – a complex, life-altering road movie.

Even in music, there are re-imaginings and recordings. Kate Bush did this with her album *Director's Cut*, where she took some of her most beloved songs and re-imagined them or found their original essence. Taylor Swift reclaimed her back catalog by releasing new versions of her albums paired with songs she was forced to cut from the original releases.

After the publication of my last full-length collection, *Midnight in a Perfect World*, in 2018, I knew the next book would highlight the 30 years that have made up my so-called "career" in poetry. This collection puts a period – a full stop – to a very long journey that has now come to a close.

But I didn't want a traditional new & selected. I wanted to mix the old and the new to tell a deeper story. I thought this was going to be my "Joan Didion LA collection," but as it was coming together, I realized that it was more about my dear uncle, Terry Graves, my beloved friend Christopher Jason Siddons, and my muse Derek Jarman – three of the millions lost to AIDS.

I grew up in the '80s as the genocide of AIDS was allowed to ravage the gay community by callous, uncaring politicians like Reagan and Thatcher. The specter of HIV/AIDS clouded my coming out, my sexual freedom, and took the people I loved. Most of the poetry I've written about AIDS has never been collected in one volume but scattered across collections and chapbooks or appeared in journals.

Rather than siloing the old and new into separate sections, the poems weave together a more complete story. Poems like "New Car Smell" (which I stupidly cut from *Render*) and "At Lake Forest Plaza" (which should have been in *Midnight*…) are now part of a richer, deeper tapestry. My collections and chapbooks have always felt like chapters in a long story, so now that story is all here in one volume. And along with what has come before are the new poems chronicling my mother's death from cancer and my own diagnosis less than two years later. The LA poems are here, the cinema and music-inspired ones, and the spirit of Anne Sexton, too.

Some of these poems have been altered to fit this narrative, heighten a mood, and create a stronger connection point. There is a prevalence of truth in my poetry, but there is also a dose of revisionist history, cinematic license, and like Lillian Hellman in *Julia*, a touch of pentimento.

I have said in numerous interviews that I am an unabashed, unashamed, unrelenting "confessional poet." Never has that been more apparent than in this volume. This book has also, finally, given me a sense of closure. While I don't think this will be my final collection, I feel like I've reached a stopping point. I find myself no longer interested in the "poetry business" of submitting to publications, applying for grants, setting up readings, or wringing my hands over who will publish the next book. With *Wonder & Wreckage*, I say goodbye to all that.

We have embarked…

Collin Kelley
February, 2024

OVERTURE

The Beat of Black Wings

They said when you got here,
the whole thing started.
Who are you? What are you?
Where did you come from?
I think you're the cause of all this.
I think you're evil!

      — Hysterical Mother in diner from Alfred Hitchcock's The Birds, 1963

Someone must always take the blame – whoring flight attendants or government bureaucrats, for example – but in this case it happens to be a cool blonde, maybe too icy in mint green, trailed by rumors from across the sea, dancing naked in a fountain, causing a scene. Because if there's no culpability, the world will spin off its axis, rotated by millions of flapping wings.

It begins in the big city, but that's too obvious, so take the action north to Bodega Bay, the tranquility ripe for destruction, the "it can't happen here" placidness broken only by seagull cries, as they wheel and dive over the harbor. And then one attacks, draws blood. Melanie Daniels, the stranger in town, becomes patient zero.

Soon, the birds are massing outside the door, indiscriminate beaks nibbling at schoolteachers and children, ruining birthday parties, upsetting casual lunches and commerce. They perch in the most unexpected places; wake up with morning wood, hazy about whether it's your wife or boyfriend next to you, and find beady eyes staring back ready to put the peck in pecker.

No one is safe, not even farmers, chain-smoking schoolmarms or overbearing mothers with retinas stronger than any contraceptive. Handsome men who spend too much time in the city with hoods and ne'er-do-wells, come home with soiled underwear and reeking of jazz and liquor, are also in mortal danger.

Realization sets in far too late, not until the air is filled with murders of crows. They wait, patient jinxes, until you're lulled into a false sense of security then attack. In the end, Melanie is drawn to the bedroom, left wide-eyed and ravaged, and the townspeople will say she got what she deserved for bringing the scourge upon them. But the radio crackles with news: the beat of black wings all the way to San Francisco.

1.
THE PARALLAX VIEW

A Broken Frame

The photograph has no date,
but these are my long-ago kin,
ancestors just before the boat,
six stone-faced on the English shore,
sepia on cardstock under glass
still clear in severe, dark clothes
except one, who has been marked
out, maybe with black wax,
which runs to the bottom corner
where the frame is cracked.

Did he die in transit, get lettered
for adultery on that long crossing,
gamble away starting-over money,
or was he the child they could no
longer bear, the ruin of the family?
The one who kissed other boys,
should have been left behind,
whose black ghost gave up
the dream, slipped out of the picture
through a broken place, a sliver.

Wonder Woman

The day I told my parents I wanted to trade in
G.I. Joe for Wonder Woman must have set off alarms.
I wanted to surrender my guns for the golden lasso;
more than the dolls, mind you, I wanted to be
Wonder Woman.
I don't remember who stitched the costume:
blue underwear with glued-on stars, a red bustier
wrapped around my seven-year-old sunken chest,
the golden eagle oddly deflated,
the headband and bullet-deflecting cuffs made
of cardboard and the length of rope my father had
spray-painted gold in the yard hooked at my side.
I lassoed my poor dad first, demanded the truth,
but there was no magic in those rough, twisted fibers.
If the rope could have squeezed out an ounce
of what he was really thinking,
I would have been dressed up as Superman or Batman,
a manly cape flying out behind me as I ran
around the backyard, hidden from the neighbors,
while my dad devised a way to build
Wonder Woman's invisible plane.

Funtown

— Stewart Avenue, Atlanta, 1974

Abandoned putt-putt golf course
on a street that will eventually
become prostitute stroll —
a picture of me at age five
hugging the flaking remains
of a dinosaur on the fourth green.
Pre-historic houses choked
with weeds, Astroturf buckling
and bleached, water features
gone dry before I was born.
And next to me is Uncle Terry,
our last visit before he packed
up and moved to San Francisco
with his boyfriend, before AIDS,
before memento mori meant
anything to him or me.
My parents say this photo —
this memory — does not exist.
But I am certain we were there,
squinting in the glare
the halo of sunspots around us
transferring the life
he would not finish on to me
so seamlessly I misremember
where our lives intersect.

Breaking My Mother's Leg

Just off the back porch,
I splashed happily in my kiddie pool
until a Godzilla-sized grasshopper
jumped in to enjoy a summer soak.

After my scream pierced the humid air,
my mother burst through the screen door
and dove from the top step.
The judges would have given her 10s
for her somersault over the shallow water,
but she couldn't stick the landing.

When I recovered, my mother
was half in, half-out of the pool
reclining like a bathing beauty,
but then I saw her right leg, twisted
at an unnatural angle, and her smile of relief
that I had not drowned turned to frown
as her eyes followed mine.

She would wear a cast to her thigh
for the rest of the summer, perfecting invalid,
and she would never be the same again.
After the cast came off, she lived a lifetime in five years,
casting my father off for another man,
flaunting herself around town.

The sharp crack of bones
was a dividing line between one life and the next,
a grace period before a host of maladies set in –
ruptured ulcers, impacted teeth and crippling stroke –
a storm that never rained itself out.

Squelch

Breaker one-nine, breaker one-nine,
staccato slang for speed traps,
Smokey and greasy spoons.
Blame it on Burt and Sally —
sexy in souped-up Trans-Am,
illegal beer, thrill of the hunt.
Hot plastic cupped in hand,
lips pressed close,
my mother's whispery voice
sending the scent of eager beaver
across three counties:
This is Foxy Lady, who's got their ears on?

We let the devil in that day,
antenna rising like a white flag
over boondock house.
My mother's new addiction: a black box
glowing on kitchen counter, hotter than any stove.
Her universe reduced to meters, huddled
in a chair, castaway connected to civilization.
Her static and crackle louder than my father,
his extraneous noise dialed out in the squelch.

We would lose meals and time
in channel-hopping void, disembodied voices
fading in and out of our lives except one,
Desperado, whose voice sent meter into red,
my mother into glittery jittery glee.
Her call and response like Marilyn singing
Happy Birthday every day to dead presidents,
until my father's head snapped back one night,
catching their rock n' roll hoochie coo,
smashing microphone into linoleum.
But by then a strange Camaro was cruising
our twenty and mom was wearing lipstick again.

Parallel Lines

My mother's mother, the one I called Moom Moom so often as a
baby that it became her nickname, dances around her kitchen to
Blondie singing *Heart of Glass* on the radio. It's 1979 and Debbie and
the boys have sold out to disco, but the mainstream doesn't care.
Dancers scream whenever the DJ spins it at the clubs, that's what
my grandmother says as she teaches me The Hustle on cracked
linoleum, her new husband claps along, can't take his eyes off her.
Moom Moom is re-married to a trucker, divorced my one-handed,
alcoholic grandfather as soon as the nest emptied, tired of the gun
in her face, waking up marinated in his drunken piss. She likes long
hauls, seeing the world, while my mother turns bitter and adulter-
ous, no sizzle in the bacon my father brings home. I stay up all night
to watch Blondie on the *Midnight Special*, learn Debbie's shawl dance
with a ripped bed sheet, purloined heels, face smeared with lipstick,
sucking a candy cigarette, mother's whereabouts unknown.

Girl Crush

—for Farrah

I grew my hair and feathered it for you,
we were the same shade of blonde.
I had the red bathing suit poster
on my bedroom wall, your smile
a nightlight, signal to noise.

Now I can see that your teeth
were clenched, head thrown back,
not so much playful as predatory,
eyes telegraphing that the tingling
I felt down below was fleeting.

There would be no compromise
after this image. You refused to take
Charlie's calls or jiggle and giggle
your way to stereotype.
That smile said, set me on fire.

Expectations defied burn faster,
consume in a crackling wave.
Love remains but is transferred.
The curve of your breast said,
I am not a mirror. Look elsewhere.

Roosters & Hens

Rumors fly fast in southern towns, like the one about my grand-
father shacked up with a sixteen-year-old he found hitchhiking to
Florida on New Year's Eve. He'd be in jail today, front page news and
cancelled, but in 1981 rural Georgia, it's just more grist for the gossip
mill. He parades Missy — his "little gal" — at the gas station, five
and dime, buys her milkshakes at the Dairy Queen, makes her go in
the store to buy his six-packs and cigarettes.

The day he brings her to my house, my mother stands cross-armed
and disgusted in the driveway as they argue over his indiscretion.
Missy sits in the car snapping her gum and singing along to "Here
You Come Again" on the radio. "I've got that 45," I say shyly, lean-
ing in the window. Her eyes light up, she looks me up and down,
reassessing my worth. "Dolly is my idol. I want to be just like her —
boobs and all!"

Only four years separate us, but Missy, in her tight jeans, tank top
and tall blonde hair, seems much older. Worldly and wise, sure of
herself, and when she casually asks me if I've ever kissed a boy, I feel
seen for the first time. Missy tells me absolutely nothing, changes
the subject when I ask about her family, school, or where she's from.

My grandfather drops us off at the movie theater to see *9 to 5*. Missy
slings an arm around my shoulder as we sing along loudly to Dolly's
theme song. I can feel the other moviegoers staring, tutting and
harrumphing their disapproval. When the scene where Mr. Hart
chases Doralee around his desk and she threatens to get the gun out
of her purse and shoot his dick off, Missy laughs and claps. "That's
just like your granddaddy, but he ain't caught me yet." Our eyes meet
in the dark and even at twelve, her implication is unmistakable.
"You'll just have to shoot him then," I say. "I won't tell." Her shrieking
laugh brings a chorus of "shhhhs" and I taste her bubblegum lipstick
for hours after she kisses me unexpectedly on the lips.

Missy is gone by spring. She disappears into the night with an envelope full of social security cash and grandpa's gun, doesn't leave a note. He rages for days, duped and lonely, begs mom for money to buy his Pabst tall boys.

I don't tell them that Missy made one last stop before she left town. The morning after her disappearance, I find a small brown bag propped on the windowsill of my room. Inside is the 45 of *9 to 5* with big-haired, busty Dolly on the sleeve marching off to work carrying a paint roller like a staff, a garden hoe, blueprints, jumper cables, work boots, and other odd job tools slung over her back. I've lost track of how many times I've watched *9 to 5*, spoken Dolly's dialogue back to the tv, and wondered if Missy ever had to use my grandfather's gun, turned any roosters into hens to get where she was going.

Knoxville: Summer, 1982

100 degrees at the World's Fair
the Sunsphere shimmers
a giant lollipop that loses
its flavor in one lick.

We sit in a cheap motel room
flipping through unfamiliar TV
our sweat-soaked clothes
stiffening in the over-chilled air.

No one speaks.

Her abandoned lover 236 miles away
my mother watches the phone
a pot that will never boil again
reaches for it, then withdraws.

Back home, Bruce jerks off
without me in his dark basement
fantasizes about cocktease Karen
decides my hand is not enough.

Dad wants to see the body farm
bones picked clean of worries
free of cheats, brats and bills
his 43rd birthday goes unmentioned.

That night I dream the Sunsphere
is a Magic 8 Ball in my hand
I shake it hard, but the same message
always floats to the surface:

better not tell you now.

At Southlake Mall

My parents made up while I was in Spencer's Gifts
examining fart in a can and hopping cocks,
waiting for other boys to finish flipping through
posters of half-naked women and sports cars.
Greasy fingerprints all over Daisy Duke's cleavage
on sale for 1.99 rolled and bagged, long and stiff.

They sat on a bench by a gurgling fountain, holding hands,
making googly eyes and sipping from the same slushie.
Even then, I wondered what she had promised.
What would erase the image of her naked legs
wrapped around another?
The lover sent running with clothes in hand
to his oversexed Camaro, face bloodied, while my father
slapped my mother repeatedly in the bathroom,
so she could see his cuckold departing in dirty mirror.

With unsigned divorce papers on the dining room table,
my parents devolved back to earlier selves,
teenagers in love, giddy with necking, third base diddling.
They couldn't wait to get home, made me eat my giant pretzel
in the backseat, her hand on his thigh as the Ford shuddered
in excess speed.

While they fucked their way back to middle class malaise,
I shot my wad all over Daisy's mid-section, would never
hang her in my room, just roll her wet and sticky under the bed
for future abuse, the same place I kept a shoplifted People,
Christopher Atkins bulging from his Blue Lagoon loin cloth,
his face and abs wrinkled from my salty spray.

After Adultery

Mother marches down the long driveway,
kicks up dust like the Tasmanian Devil,
rocks spit from under her sure steps.
She carries cutting shears like a rifle
into battle against two monster hedges,
overgrown sentinels, embarrassments
weighing heavily on her empty dance card.
She attacks the first bush with pent up vengeance,
blades flash in midday sun, shorn leaves
tornado around her head until she's swallowed.
Then the hedge becomes space alien,
and I can hear my mother curse it
like Ripley on the *Sulaco*, egging it on,
calling it a bitch like the roots will answer.

The rash appears that night, covers her
entire body, no region left untouched
by bumps and red streaks.
She becomes unhinged, snatches hair
then a snake naked and striking on bathroom floor.
And we, conscripted caretakers, become targets
for her poison, forked tongue as she floats
Ophelia-style in the tub, water simmering,
her eyes fixed and distant,
as if she has finally found the tesseract,
the wrinkle in time, folding space behind her
so we cannot follow, leaving us
with a crazed shadow, a white devil woman.

Physical Education

I push my ass back against him,
feel his hand go slack at my throat,
subtle shifting of power as he grows
hard against my tighty-whiteys,
settling into unexplored crack,
we find empty locker room rhythm.

When the coach returns unexpectedly,
David pinballs off benches, struggling
into his too-tight Jordache jeans
and cable knit sweater, pre-come
oozing through boxers, a bead
of sweat dangling off his nose.

I stand there watching, pious
in my t-shirt and Fruit of the Looms,
flaccid and un-aroused, lording
over his secret desires coaxed out
from behind year-old bully screen
and titty-twister fingers.

In PE he will never look at me again,
too busy hiding his sudden boner
from the other boys who jeer,
call him faggot, and I could save him
with one limp wrist, but this is junior high,
and the smell of blood is in the air.

Xenomorphs

After break-up and make-up,
my parents took me to see *Aliens*.
R-rated treat for being a brave little soldier.
No xenomorphs could match
the double-jawed bite and acid tongue
of my mother and father in protracted battle.
I had put myself in stasis
to stop my chest from bursting.

As the reel unfurled Ripley's nightmare,
I shed another layer of skin,
put one foot in the aisle,
white-knuckled the armrests for dust off.
Every man for himself.
I was almost sixteen.
The space between us would be vast.

First Gay Crush

Dirk was the name of my first gay crush,
goddamn how I lusted after that nerdy fuck.
I was 15 almost 16 and he was 18 going on 19,
and I was the prom queen hot for college cock.
His mismatched clothes, ill-fitting jeans, dirty sneakers,
my queer eye for a sexually confused guy already razor sharp.
I was too young to know I had control,
that my aim was true and his was scattershot
from years of strict military parenting.

We would sit in his dorm room
listening to Kate Bush records
and watching *Doctor Who* on PBS.
I let my hand stray to touch his thigh, rest there
until he flinched as if flicked by holy water.
My father thought Dirk and I were fucking
after he caught me on the phone at 1 a.m.
in the dark living room.
Oh, Daddy, if only.
He would never come out of the closet for me.

Last night, I dreamed I met Dirk again in a coffee shop.
I saw him through the window, dark hair falling over his eyes,
his perfect white teeth a beacon.
I was thin again, like those last two years of high school
when I starved myself better than any cheerleader,
wearing a black coat tight at the waist.
I slid into the booth next to him and he kissed me, unafraid.
When I woke, all I could think about was the night
I told him I was gay and had fallen in love with someone else.
He gripped the steering wheel and stared straight ahead,
driving us into oncoming headlights.
"What," he screamed. "What do you want me to do about it?"

Suicide 17

I committed suicide at 17, left a note folded in my car on a late October morning, my knuckles cold against frosty windshield as I pressed the paper to the dash. I parked my car in the high school lot, left the doors unlocked. I was riding with three other classmates to a university workshop, but I would not be coming home. I would leap from a rooftop, walk in front of a bus, selfishly snatch the steering wheel into oncoming traffic.

I left words for the boy I was desperately in love with, who was also poor and from a broken home. He followed me relentlessly, but would never let me in. I would sit on his bed, watch him undress, try not to stare. He would accidentally brush against me over and over, daring me to make the first move. I didn't blame the boy. I just wanted him to know that I removed the elephant from the room, solved the unanswerable puzzle of us. He would try suicide later, sitting in his car on a snowy side street, confessing to my ghost as the love I had for him fogged the windows. It was always winter between us.

I wanted to die that day and I did. At the hands of a frat boy who kissed me on a dark landing in the student center as I contemplated hurling myself down the stairs. He stood over me with a cigarette dangling from his lips, asking me back to his room, telling me I was beautiful. I did not go with him, but I stood up out of my body and kicked it down the stairs, flew into that other boy's arms, tasted his smoky breath, his hands all over me, his hardness exploding against my leg. Then I walked over my corpse and did not look back. I have never again wanted to die as much as I did that day when I was 17.

The note lay on my dash all day long, crinkled from the damp morning, turned crisp by the sun. I held it in my hands, read the words as a stranger would. Grieved for the loss, thankful it wasn't me.

Sex In My Parents' House

I was 19 before I had sex in my parents' house. Serious sex, not exploratory masturbation with Bruce, my first best friend, when we were 12 and naked in the woods behind his house. What would Mom and Dad have done if they had found me face down on the living room floor? Lee's ass pumping air, deep drilling, the baby blue shag carpet giving me rug burns. Lee, who I treated badly because he was just a stand in for the one who got away, breath laden with *I love you's* that were more than just orgasms talking.

Later, I feigned insanity, indifference, incompatibility to make him go away. Could hear the hurt in his voice over the phone and wished I could snatch rejection back down the snake-coiled line twisted like a tourniquet around my arm. No one has ever made love to me quite like Lee did those short months we were together. He was an adult, knew how to please, wanted to please me, tried over and over. My mother liked Lee, said he was pretty, would have forgiven the stains on the carpet, the image of her son impaled on the floor in the room we only used when company came.

I can still smell that carpet, old and dusty with disuse, stretching out before me like a cartoon ocean. I floated upon it, disembodied, seeing what my parents might see from the doorway. The truth they had always known, no longer at the edge of their thoughts, but overtaking them like a baby blue shag tidal wave.

New Car Smell

My first memory of riding in a car
was in my father's 1965 Plymouth Belvedere,
sandwiched between him and my mother
on the vinyl bench, before the law
required belts or backseat banishment.

I would pick at the yellow foam bursting
from the jagged crack between my legs,
my father swearing he'd fix it,
my mother rolling her eyes.

One day, I found him in the carport
on his knees in Bermuda shorts
beside the open passenger door of his beloved
Belvedere, the first new car he'd ever owned,
mixing up a can of vinyl repair.
He spread the hot goo over the tear, smoothed
it like cake icing, cursed under his breath.
This shit won't work.

I used to run my fingers over the raised skin
of this home remedy, differentiating texture
where the old vinyl and new met, slowly
picking at it, being told to quit
over and over again, but by then
other cracks were appearing.

Before my father became frail, before
dialysis and blindness, he sold the car,
no room in the driveway, my mother's
consolation gunboat taking up too much space.
He stuffed the $300 into his pocket
without counting it, watched some redneck
haul it away, a carcass, a faded memory
of time before me, when a new car, my young mother
sitting pretty at the drive-in made him king.

My father bought a new truck, we sat in the cab,
admiring bells and whistles, I told him
new car smell is one of the best scents in the world.
He shook his head. *It's not the same.*

In Stockholm

When she can walk again without assistance,
my mother refuses further rehab, subverts nurses
with her twisted mouth, a profane voice
that climbs operatically in anger and despair.
Even after the doctors diagnose brain damage,
pre-existing insanity, urge commitment,
my father cannot sign the papers.

The mere suggestion that she seek help
makes her bare teeth, her eyes flash,
one good arm still agile enough to jerk
tubes out of veins, hurl anything in reach.
She demands her pocketbook, the beginning
of a new obsession, as if by holding purse strings
tight enough she can keep her freedom.

This paranoia will continue like a siege
and while money will become her chief concern,
keeping tabs on me and my father will come
a close second, phone lines crackling with rage,
a one-woman FBI tracking our every move,
time-clocking our lives to the second,
and if the answers don't chime with her busted
inner gears, an acid tongue hysteria returns.
From this moment on, everything –
from flat tires to thunderstorms – will be our fault,
another instance of us bleeding her dry.

Like Patty Hearst, we will adapt, acquiesce,
sometimes sympathize, stop asking why.

Spring Hill

—Midtown Atlanta, 1993

Spring Street where it crosses 10th,
the funeral home corner,
where they handed Uncle Terry back
in a cardboard box.
Reduced him, made him fit
in a ziplock bag, made him volcano
dust and bone chips.
AIDS made him Pompeii.

In a yellowed newspaper 1951,
the births and deaths side by side,
Terry's name appeared opposite
a photo of that same corner.
The white walls and gabled roof,
iv-veined portico for private tears,
biding its time, unchanged
save for the mourners' faces
and the bodies of those beautiful boys.

One day, I'll be taken to that corner,
so I take a good, long look,
memorize each brick,
in case the soul is blind or refuses to hover,
or if death is only blackness and I am just ashes.

Christmas Day

Dad has gone blind,
every mouthful of food a surprise
as his fork moves uncertainly
over the holiday meal.
He stands unsteadily, waiting
for blood to circulate back to his feet
before shambling back to the living room.
He lingers in front of the old gas heater,
wavers like the blue jets flickering in the grate,
says he's never warm.

Mom is a demented tour guide,
pointing out photos I've seen hundreds
of times in my grandmother's house,
a shrine to Uncle Terry, dead ten years,
who makes the electric lights shimmer
whenever we mention his name.
We exchange unwanted gifts and cash,
find solace in this routine, make excuses
for why it isn't more – the dwindling
social security checks or doctor bills.

Small talk will turn to accusations,
to nitpicking, to shortcomings.
Grandmother will retreat to the kitchen,
put on yellow gloves, plunge into hot dishwater
until the air returns to normal, until overfull bellies
sedate us into submission, the need for naps,
so she can usher us out, mission accomplished,
with a forced, *don't be a stranger.*

Mom will say, *it doesn't feel like Saturday*,
because holidays are always inscrutable,
like rooms with no clocks or windows
and time that flattens out into dead air.
We are suspended here, holding our breath,
waiting for the world to spin again on its axis.

2.
FIRE WALK WITH ME

Firewater

— for Chris

Back door, old house.
Snow melting faster
than paper burns.
And some child
is running in the woods.
He is at my side now.
Kissing my face,
holding my hands.
Bitterly cold, he
half naked.
I lead him to the couch,
lay him down, smother
him with my body.
Kisses, apologies,
promises...forgotten.
Ghost.
He melts through my veins
like firewater.
And passes through my
soul as winter does.

The realization of rain

Make it rain inside this room.
I see moving pictures, grey screen,
dresses trailing in mud.
A distorted sound of thunder,
a muffled sound of rain falling
in colorized meadows.
From every corner, shadows inch
like rising damp, running down my face.
Rain is never ugly there,
even as it drowns the earth.
Press a hand against the picture,
all slick and flat.
Rain has a way of falling inside your head,
a constant reminder.
It never rained a single day you were here,
now all it does is pour.
In this picture room, we watched drops fall
on others a world away.
A shared fantasy of making love in a storm.
Situations deteriorate rapidly,
water washing away the beachhead.
The corrosion is soft and steady.
One more memory in the jar.
I can see it distorted and bloated,
like looking through a teardrop.
When we speak of these days
of rain, we will mark a passage.
When I put my pen to paper,
nothing will smear out the words.
Days will pass into night, unnoticed,
with only clocks to keep the difference.

Riot

— for TJ

Last night I remembered 1992,
that spring night I drove you home
with a butcher knife on my lap.
You lived in an unsafe neighborhood,
the TV and radio said Los Angeles
was on fire and we were next.
But the verdict was in:
I could only think of you.

Of getting you into my bed
for 15 minutes before you had to be home.
We existed on a diet of sweat, cum
and the hunger pains of separation.
Our furtive nights together were so few
and far between that the night LA burned,
we stopped to fuck in the parking lot of a church,
but there was no sanctuary involved.

Shadows moved from every direction,
sounds of distant sirens, too-close voices,
a gunshot to heighten our unrest.
We would disintegrate in a few weeks,
the clandestine affair wearing us down
to accusations and tears.

I can still see that blade propped on the dash,
within easy reach, the thrill of potential
discovery and death fogging the windows.
I can still see, reflected in the knife's edge,
the image of you going down on me
for the last time.

At Lake Forest Plaza

— East New Orleans

The hotel is a skeleton,
whitewashed ribs, its name a shadow
etched into the wall like nuclear flash.
Read Blvd. is just one ground zero,
I-10 a gallery of ruin.
My memory is long.

I first came here on the run from Chris,
when he was alive and crazy,
unwinding the double helix of us,
embarrassed by his public madness.
I wanted to sweat him out anonymously,
heat cure for lingering malady.

I could only afford the outskirts,
but I had memorized the map
so Canal, Vieux Carre, Carondelet,
St. Charles, Garden District
were second tongue, steeped
in Tennessee, Truman, Ignatius
and Julie Marsden in a red dress
at the Olympus Ball.

This is 1992, dumplin', 1992, not the Dark Ages.

I learned to acclimate, even found
charm in the Lake Forest Plaza Mall,
its food court a cheap haven
when I could find pleasure in nothing.
Chris and money burning holes
in my pockets, finally going for broke —
Maison Blanche, mon amour.

On TV, helicopters hovered
over the flooded mall, waist-deep

black water, tattered roof waving
white flags and although it had been
10 years since I'd set foot there,
my hand traced the places
where I'd walked to shake Chris off.

I should have called him then,
when he was alive and not crazy.
I know that now, driving past the place
where the mall used to stand, swept
off the earth as if some angry god's hand
descended and cleared a table.

The rain children

I dream of my forehead against streetcar window,
cool vibration and constant motion.
Car empty, I move from seat to seat, see all sides.
Late summer, tourists are gone, I have this ride to myself.
The driver does not speak, does not stop, as we glide
through the Garden District toward the river, lost in reverie.

Along the levee, I contemplate the motion of water,
where it could take me, walk against the current,
and wind-whipped horizontal rain.

At St. Louis Cathedral, water heavy in my clothes,
pulling me to my knees, giving in to genuflection.
I place palms on the cool stone, and distantly
there is thunder, but the sound is swallowed whole.

Kneeling in a little drowning pool, I recall your face,
your deep-sea diver eyes, other places I have drowned.
Down the street we would dance, bodies wound together,
your hair, your lips, our tongues entwined.
I loved you more than I would ever say.
Now you are gone, swirling away like water down a drain
marked N.O.

I have been drenched before, in other places, by other rain,
but only this place opens its watery arms to embrace me,
with its soft, slow days, its enveloping heat, the Morse code
of raindrops tapping along Rue St. Ann.

I am one more of the rain children, who found their way south
in despair, was baptized in sky tears, absolved of you, turned
you into poetry, a sharp horn note for jazz funeral.

Credentials

I sit at a table with four famous poets,
but only one acknowledges my existence.
I am here by chance, a generous offer from
the one who heard me read the night before.
But it is the man who studies me like something
scraped from the bottom of his shoe who asks
the question: *What are your credentials?*

I have not been published in The New Yorker,
Kenyon, Atlantic, Poetry or Paris Review.
Just a few credits to my name in
small *magazines*, journals, online.
This stammered response is not enough.
Will never be enough. I am in my Jesus year,
and I am crucified at a greasy spoon by someone
with a wall full of degrees, five books and an ego
that sucks life from the room. I am 33 years old
and I do not have the proper credentials.
I am not worthy to be at the table and the shifting
of his body away from me ends any hope.
He will not speak to me again that evening and
I will not write a word for a week,
burn myself down for not having thought of the words
to say, to come back at him. They come later,
perfect and ineffectual. They always do.

I am the legacy of parents who put their
game faces at my late birth and wear them to this day.
Poker faces that sent me reeling into the world,
searching for emotions and signals and needs
yet to be satiated.
I survived two boys who stripped me of my sense
of self so they could create their own.
I lived through years of raised hands,
threats to leave and threats to return,
ran into those arms like an un-tethered animal

too stupid to be stunned by the stick.
I sat at the same desk for 12 years writing
innocuous words for others while my own words
circled my neck like a noose.
Choking on their need for release only to find
they were not good enough.
I took every rejection in stride, paying my dues,
waiting for that spark that would transcend words
into poetry.

Even after some modicum of success, someone
was always there to temper it.
What journals have you appeared in?
Who will publish your book?
I will do it myself like Whitman and countless
others before and after him. But it is not enough.
It does not have that scent of academia and cliques,
a rarefied air.
Whitman was a hundred years ago, a fluke,
an accepted anomaly.
They say I missed my chance when I dropped
out of college because I could not afford tuition,
could not focus enough for remedial algebra.

On many days, I have struggled just to stay.
Resisting urges to swallow stashed pills,
sitting in the garage with the door closed,
Fleetwood Mac playing on the radio,
lulling me to sleep in the backseat,
fumes merging with a song from my childhood.

My god, man.
You have the nerve to ask for my credentials
when I am sitting here before you. Alive.

Saving Anne Sexton

Because she saved me once, it's the least I can do.
There was a note left at my door, scribbled in haste,
about where to make the exchange.
A $117 ransom to save Anne from unworthy hands.
I imagine her bound inside a box, waiting it out
in a dark warehouse for early morning rescue.

I arrive early, the pink paper clutched in my grip.
I park inside a gate, walk up a ramp, ring a buzzer.
A window snaps up and an arm extends.
I put the paper in the open palm and it draws back.
Minutes later, the box is pushed across to me,
larger than I expected, and the window closes again.
I rush the box back to my car, cut the tape
with my dull key until I find her bound and gagged
in masking tape and bubble wrap under wadded-up
newspapers from New Hampshire.

Anne is pristine for all her travels, like three decades
have not separated us, like you never died when I was five.
The Book of Folly is stamped on her in red and black,
the words she made her business tucked inside.
I gently open the cover and see her signature,
imagine your wrist touching those gilded edges,
trace the big A and S, the x that marks the spot.

This is a rescue 30 years too late, and I know
she would say, smoke curling from her cigarette,
that I saved the best part, the things that kept her up
at night now sitting on my shelf safe from harm.

Peter Greenaway

Our worlds collide over music and poetry.
In this familiar city where I planned suicide
and your girlfriend was raped.
I lived, you turned to men, almost died,
the chemo killing you faster than the cancer.
We are both in remission.

You love the absurdity and uncertainty
of Peter Greenaway films:
the changing colors of Helen Mirren's dress,
the treachery of numbers and skipping rope,
the insanity of architecture.
The critics wouldn't understand us either.

We are stranger than fiction,
we color outside the lines,
we speak on the phone long distance
as if communicating from different continents.
You are further north, closer to London,
the place we both agree on,
the place we could happily succumb to:
the music, literature, cinemas on every corner
where we could sit all day.
The proximity of our shoulders electric,
your hand on my inner thigh the center of the universe.
These joys un-numbered, living some other life,
answerable only to the whim of fate,
giving ourselves up to uncertainty.

We get into the leaking boat, row out,
taking on water.
Holding hands as we slip into the blackness.
Cheating death at our leisure, surrendering
to that perfect finite weight.

At Prospect Cottage

— for Derek Jarman

Stone beach in September, where it's always sweater weather, the gloom glare blinds, sky and sea merge. My feet sink in shingle, ankles turn. The empty lighthouse, humming power station rise on the headland, and in the marshes three listening ears, massive and manmade acoustic mirrors, aimed at the channel, bouncing sound waves from invading aircraft. Alien and alienating.

Derek saw the beauty in the desolation, the quietest place in England, the opposite of London where the thrum of infected blood often pounded more loudly in his ears than the traffic. The prospect of writing one last film, one last poem, planting one last flower. The challenge of bloom in the rock – if he could make something grow here then anything was possible. Maybe another chance, another life. Opium poppy for pain, red valerian for insomnia, devil's-bit for coughs and fevers.

Etched into the cottage wall, along notebook-ruled slats, Donne's "The Sunne Rising" admonishes the interruption of light on lovers entwined in bed. I imagine Derek inside the black and yellow hive as his world turned blue, daydreaming of space, chanting the names of dead lovers he would soon join.

Twenty years since he succumbed, the same year Uncle Terry shook off flesh gravity, I lean against the weathered boat and remember them both. In my pocket, a smooth pebble and fading bloom, something to take home for worry and press, my souvenirs from the place Derek called paradise.

In Tavistock Square

— after Mrs. Dalloway

I am sleeping in the corner of your ghost house, Virginia,
your Blitz-bombed house now a hotel full of rooms,
not of one's own, but for a parade of neverending strangers.

I rub my hand over your hard, slick head in the square
wet with summer rain, your hawkish nose turned toward
the other bombsite, the metal bus a twisted bloom of blood.

Dickens wrote *Hard Times* on the other side of the trees
and I find that living here is hard and has no time
for idealistic, broke dreamers. He wrote *Bleak House* there, too.

I am stubborn, Virginia. I come back again and again
even as this city pulls me close and pushes me away,
in love with bellow and uproar; London; this moment of June.

Perhaps I should reconsider the scattering of my ashes,
commit them to the breeze that blows through Bloomsbury.
Make me fertilizer; plaster; eye grit; nowhere; everywhere.

The view from Agnes' flat

100 steps up a steep Victorian
staircase, gasping at every landing,
sweat puddling behind my ears,
the effort to lift body weight vertically
more difficult every year.

But the coronary is worth it,
because out the window
is a travel brochure come to life:
Christopher Wren's dome
against gleaming modernity,
the sounds of traffic and voices
mixing with the coos and cries.

I will never live here,
but the room is always mine.
Sometimes you have to adapt,
take what you can get,
appreciate the view.

Atonement

I am sitting in a London cinema watching Vanessa Redgrave make
amends for a life of deceit, to a soundtrack of rushing water I believe
subliminal, to drive home melancholy, but when silhouetted heads
turn in search, I realize it is real. It is raining hard outside, echoing
behind the screen, and suddenly your death comes rushing back to
me, Christopher, whom I have not mourned.

Fifteen years ago, we watched Vanessa give away *Howards End*,
thrilled at elegant despair and handwringing, the way the rain never
looked ugly there, was always just enough and never too much.
When our sweaty young palms found each other's in the dark, our
dreams came in fast whispers, the promise that we would go to
London one day.

I am here now, Christopher, and I feel you near. I am writing these
words for you in
Leicester Square, the English rain cold and perfect on my skin, yet
the ink does not smear. You will not let me forget so easily, although
I have tried to make you a stranger, a casualty of your own vices.

My fear is that I passed you on the street, when you were homeless
and addicted, unrecognizable ghetto scarecrow, invisible and all
the same, part of the city landscape. Maybe you were behind the
gas station in a cold sweat, shooting meth to forget the HIV shame.
Swallowed up in pride.

Your death is a voicemail, left by another with a phone number. The
somber tone is unmistakable, a hush earmarked for the dead. Four
days gone – long enough to have shaken off flesh gravity – I expect
your ghost to rattle the unearthly chains of your discontent. Even
when I skip the memorial, numb on the couch as twilight approach-
es, picking the memory of you like a scab, I realize that you are not
so much a wound, but a scar that will never fade.

But today, you come back as the sound of rain and fill me up like a bucket until I brim. Not a dry eye in the house, anyway. So clever, you, subtle and un-paranormal. I mourn you with celluloid, Christopher, in dark rooms where stories unfurl, with rushing water, with a city that pulls me near and pushes me away, with clocks that always know the score.

In the afterlife my father is a London cab driver

The hotel concierge gestures toward the waiting taxi, its back door
already open. I slide in, say good morning, and an American voice
speaks back. Unmistakably my father, dead three days, smiling at
me in the rearview mirror as he pulls into traffic on Bayswater Road.
There's no destination, so we'll make a loop around Hyde Park, long
enough for him to tell me to be happy, healthy and wise – to not
give up on the dream of really being here when I wake. Leave it to
Daddy-O to leave it this way, to meet me on beloved ground he'd
only heard about from my stories or watched on TV. When I think of
my father now, he will always be in London, not gasping like a fish
in a hospital bed as his heart went still. His new chosen profession
to ferry the living between the stations of their grief, jovially tipping
his cap as he drops fares at the corner of the rest of their lives.

Meeting Jeanne Moreau

In this dream, I meet Jeanne Moreau
at the Louvre, and like Buddhas,
we sit at the feet of Aphrodite,
better known as Venus.

Goddesses come in many forms
with different faces, assuming names.
I would follow you until the end of the world,
leave a trail of lovers in our smoky wake.
Women like you are bonfires
for those who aspire to be consumed.
Dive in, full of fuel, feed the flames.
We all catch fire and burn
at the same degree of intensity.

Possessed witch or innocent virgin.
I offer myself, a willing victim.
Consider me the arson's apprentice,
the one who struck the match.
Teach me assassination, the thing you do
with your eyes and mouth that make men
take up guns.

Before I wake, the world becomes
black and white, like the first time
I saw you, shimmering out of Paris night,
gliding on Miles' jazz riff, head back,
soaking up the rain, your voice
gurgling with desire...

...je t'aime... je t'aime

The Last Confession of Sister Ruth

— Black Narcissus, 1947

On top of this mountain, the air is too thin even for God. He can't
see me out of habit, slinking down the scrabbled path, my prayer
lost in the drone and strafe of the high Himalayas. There's a man
waiting, warm-blooded, where the wind is calm. Oh, sisters, how do
you quench the fire, the lava that flows from between your thighs,
the constant reminder of past and present, the vow of untouched
future? I am a Bride of Christ, but this long-distance relationship
just isn't working out. What did I think I would find here? My life's
purpose blowing out of the snowcaps? Maybe the devil found me in-
stead. On those long, cold nights as the wind moaned desire into my
ear, a demon appeared in the mirror, put ice in my veins and murder
in my fingers. No one can stop me now. I'm going to the village to
offer myself as a sacrifice, and if that man sends me back up the
mountain, I'll just come down again — flying — wearing my forbidden
red lipstick as a beacon.

The unrequited arsonist

It's not the love itself that burns, but the hunt.
From coast to coast, tire scorch and gasoline
in my wake or chemtrails for the flyover states.
Watch and wonder where I'll come down hard,
wheels sparking tarmac, raising alarms.
I made up my mind – and yours –
left nothing for the return trip.
It was a yes or no question that set me off,
your hemming and hawing
over our future an accelerant.
This is the mystery of combustion
you will solve too late.
I'm already in your city, your street, your bed
with my hair of embers on your pillow.

Another Monica Bellucci Dream

—after Twin Peaks; for all the Davids

Last night, I had another Monica Bellucci dream.
I was in London writing a book. Monica called
and asked me to meet her at the White Horse pub.
She said she needed to talk to me.

When we met at the pub, David was there
but I couldn't see his face.

Monica was very pleasant. She had come alone.
We both had wine.

And then she said: *We're not going to talk about Paris.*
That moment has come and gone;
it is an answer with no question.

A very powerful, uneasy feeling came over me.
Monica looked out the window and indicated to me
that something was happening there. I turned and looked.
I saw myself. I saw myself from long ago
standing with David outside Covent Garden tube station.
The first time I ever came to London.

David holds me tightly and then he kisses me,
something he had never done before in public.
He says we are living inside a dream —
that we have become doppelgangers, tulpas.
We will return to the states as different people,
call each other by different names.

Nothing is the same after this.

I feel a pervasive melancholy, not only for things lost,
but of things to come that will also be lost.
I imagine my insides — intestines and stomach — cleaned out,
smooth and gleaming like new pipes

or the tub of a washing machine.
I scrub my flesh until I am a pale version of my former self.
A vestige. A cheap copy.

I go to bed hungry, chewing the inside of my cheek
until I taste blood.
My teeth are a puzzle in my mouth.

I am unrecognizable to myself.

Monica is ready to leave. She kisses me on both cheeks.
Then she asks a strange question: *Is it future or is it past?*
Now this is really something interesting to think about.
And then she says:
Oh, mio caro amico, there is fire where you're going.

ENTR'ACTE

Siege

California sunset, Ronnie's head to the west,
finally out of his ass, and Nancy's death's head
resting on the coffin, patting it
like she must have patted him
with her stranger's hands these last ten years,
his forgetfulness absolute.
You can't help but cry, the old bastard
finally dead, like a daddy who beat you
almost to death, but still there is that time
you cannot erase. Those years of silence
from the east, while the sound of blood boiling
in veins was deafening in the west.
Somehow it's fitting that they are burying him
here, in this decimated land he called home.
Where the sunset began for millions long before
he arrived draped in a flag, one he fashioned
into a noose, those old cowboy knots, and hung
over a high limb and let those California boys swing.
They brought the disease on themselves, he knew
their kind from his Hollywood days, grab-assing
in the Warner Brothers' dressing rooms. Faggots.
Bad enough he had to dirty his mouth with the word
AIDS, but gay would never pass his lips,
as if his withholding the word banished them,
made their cries of *shame, shame, shame* outside
the White House nothing more than a collective
bad dream. He made it seven years without giving in
to those bleeding heart homos, liberals and whiny doctors.
He made a joke out of untying the purse strings,
while he was a rainmaker when it came to warheads,
arms trading, terrorist training and knocking down walls.
He ended the Cold War while his own country turned to ice.

So they bury him as the day closes, the sky on fire
like the hell he'll have to talk himself out of if it exists.
Give the Devil an old song and dance, make promises,
barter with empty pockets, cast uncertain eyes skyward
at the screaming angels who lay siege to Heaven's Gate,
prepared to fall again before he's allowed to enter.
One lost kingdom is enough.

3.
PLAY IT AS IT LAYS

As the rush comes

Cecilia says my best words are yet to come,
so I wrote these slowly, died a little more in their creation.
We are all slipping away.
I unplug the clock, keep timetables for slow boats to China,
trains that travel cross country, more simple ways to live.

Everyone is eventually overtaken,
our paths littered with disappointment, heartbreak,
deaths of those we don't realize we love until they are gone.
And this will be interspersed with joy so fast you'll need
a tight net to catch and hold it for even a short time.

Cecilia flies to the coast, is writing her best words
in a breezy LA room surrounded by books, says come.
She uncorks the vessel of her travels, grief and sorrow,
lets them flow on pages, as I prepare to break the seal,
regain time and consciousness of all those things I had put away.
The clock sits un-tethered from its source and still it ticks.

Five days in LA

Things I haven't done in LA:
Met a movie star,
felt an earthquake,
had an easy commute,
been consumed by fire.

The whole city feels
make-believe, temporary
and so do the men.
Does sex count in a mirage?
When they slip away
into the night and their faces
become memory blanks
the moment the door closes
behind them?

For five days, my rented
apartment had an open
door policy and yet
it always felt empty.
Outside the windows
an audience of foragers
and nightcrawlers
watched me take all comers,
grim and expressionless.

Any city can make you
feel anonymous, but LA
erases you.
But I always come back.
Waiting to be starstruck,
shaken, easy rider,
touched by flame.

Los Angeles

The 405 sparkles like a shit-stained diamond
before me, brown smog settling over the basin,
those expensive cars, like the one I've been given,
stopping and starting in cranky first baby steps.

I can do anything, now that I've traveled these streets
alone at night, no map, just hastily scribbled directions
and places to avoid.
Traffic lights are merely suggestions,
horns are honked out of habit, for something to do,
to lull oneself out of motionlessness.
Walking In LA plays in my head like a broken record,
keeping time with a turn signal the old blue-hair
in front of me forgot to turn off.
Nobody walks in LA.

I see the sights drive-by style:
Hollywood sign, Walk of Stars, Miracle Mile.
I'm more interested in hearing about what burned
at the corner of Fairfax and Pico during the riots.
Mo' Better Meatty Meat Burgers was flame-broiled
and now that property is condemned.
The sporting goods store on Wilshire, looted with joy
and they played basketball in the parking lot
with stakes higher than any pick-up game in South Central.

Eye candy is plentiful here, everyone waiting
for their drugstore Lana Turner moment, even boys
in heels. This town makes me want to do drugs,
overdose on the common denominator.
Some blindfold falls over me as we pass the Viper Room,
where River died on the sidewalk.
I never wanted to see that place, made a vow to avoid
LA at all costs for what it cost an imperfect angel.

This city doesn't give me any vibe, no signals,
like a station off air.
Somewhere in the static, a face is trying to come through,
a movie I saw long ago or some other song, Zevon maybe.
And in the rolling vertical hold the words come clearly:
send lawyers, guns and money.

Velocity

I'm not driving the freeway, it's driving me.
In herky-jerky motions, pushing me down the 405
on a warm January night to read words for strangers.

The convergence of cars at the Garden Grove exit
may be the closest I ever come to swimming in a school of fish.
We're all floating along, some racing ahead, others falling back,
red taillights bobbing in inky darkness.

On the flyover, the road flattens out and I could easily be
floating in space, silence inside my head,
where just an hour ago, my brain was back-talking, telling me
to pack up and go home, that I'm too old, to set in my ways
for this vagabond life.

The jaundiced bathroom light turned me into a corpse,
my whole body looked bruised, teeth yellow, the mirror
super-sizing me from all directions, revealing hidden flaws.
Bad lighting is why people commit suicide in hotels.
A sound comes over the fluorescent hum, paper rustling
in the next room, my written down life calling me back.

As I tramp down the familiar freeway,
hands at the three and nine on the rented wheel,
I press hard on the gas pedal, the velocity levitating
the pages of poetry riding shotgun.
Into the night we go, shooting stars.

LA poetry reading

You are mid-poem when I arrive,
your sissy voice issuing
from lowered face, curtained
by '70s bangs, your salmon
colored shirt a size too small and
clinging to narrow frame.
Your oval nipples, ribs, belly button
a triptych of shadows
I suddenly want to lick.

You remind me of someone I cannot
remember, or maybe you're just the idea
of someone I'd like to remember.
You, maybe nineteen, would be a tentative
lover, embarrassed by your gangly body,
then emboldened by my cries of pleasure,
you'd soon roll me over and take charge,
let whiskers sprout, become a man, learn
to be jaded.

While you read, the LA wind whips
the palm tree against the window
in a rhythm I will use later when I
am alone and abusing myself, becoming
another of those crumbling people
you wish to save but can only pity.

My bowels release on Hollywood Boulevard

My sphincter gives up the fight at Hollywood and Vine,
releases a torrent of diarrhea into my underwear,
as I struggle to stuff napkins down my jeans
to stem the flow of airplane food and anxiety.

I have a *Trainspotting* moment in a dirty gas station toilet,
haunches hovering over the seat carved with gang symbols,
graffiti sharp enough to slice delicate cheeks.
Like Renton, I dream of gleaming white convenience
and sparkling taps, but as my gut spasms and squirts
I'm busy trying to figure out what to do with my soiled Calvins,
the leakage into my last pair of clean jeans.

Feet pace outside, waiting their turn, maybe doing
the dookie dance, while I try to wash out my drawers in
the rusted sink, before finally discarding them in an overflowing
trashcan. My t-shirt will hide the shit stain on my jeans
as I freeball it back to the car in search of pink relief.
I'll meditate a calm stomach all the way to Redlands,
but even as the poo crisis passes, I can hear my intestines
rumbling and roaring, ferrying another river of burning stool,
and while I try to fight it, my ass clinches in anticipation.

Crave

Looking at me, the two old daddies
lick their lips in unison, hover around
me, their fingers stroke gray beards,
recreate the sound of moth wings
slapping against lightbulb.

One tells me about his wife and kids,
but he's sodomizing me in his mind,
and the other, tall and rotund, takes
my picture for future masturbation,
un-phased by the awkward silence,
the lapse of conversation.

For a split second, I think of being
underneath them in the back of a van,
letting them ravish me as I have
done to boys half my age, who did not
want me, but wanted to know what
worship felt like, to be drunk on the
need, the shameless, hungry crave.

Whitworth Avenue, 1 a.m.

Boo
Boo
Boo Kitty
Boo Kitty
Boo Kitty Boo
Boo Boo Kitty
Kitty Boo Boo
Boo
Boo
Kitty Boo
Kitty Boo
Where are you, Boo?
Come home, Boo Kitty.

For an hour, she wanders Whitworth,
calling the lost cat.
Her voice melodic, never angry,
almost lulls me to sleep.

Boo
Boo Kitty
Boo Boo Kitty
Kitty Boo Boo
Boo Kitty Boo.

Distantly, a meow
over the indistinct
hum of the city.
Pacific breeze
billows the curtains.
Another place not my own
where I could slink away,
happily disappear
with no one to call my name.

Fucking in Long Beach

This hotel is made for sex. Mirrors on every wall, a bench under the window with a grand view of Ocean Boulevard where an Asian boy is on his knees begging me to fuck him. He waves to those watching across the way, like he's on a Macy's float, with my cock up his ass. We're the midnight show, and as I slam into him, I see fingers pointing, I see cocks appearing like dolphins leaping out of the dark Pacific, fists pumping the air, cheering us on. So, I grab the boy by the hair, pull back sharply, give the audience the rough stuff, their money's worth before the money shot, which I shoot over the boy's head onto the glowing window. And then the boy is slapping his meat against the window, gyrating like a stripper, until he unloads, guttural sounds, face contorted. We close the curtains, he dresses quickly, takes $20 for a cab, and leaves. When I go back to the window, all the watchers are gone, show over. And all that's left is to clean up the spunk, like a janitor mopping sticky floors at a porn theatre, after a night of anonymous encounters and fleeting bliss.

The woman with glass in her face

— Earthquake, 1974

She first appears in a cut crowd scene,
blue blouse, mustard bow,
handsome and middle-aged.

It's not until the earthquake is almost over
that we see her again, dodging a collapsing building,
a teenage daughter trailing behind her,
stumbling through the debris.
The girl calls out for her mom
and the woman turns her back to the camera.

That's when it happens.

From above, the sound of breaking glass,
then a guttural cry. She turns, face bloodied,
the shard embedded in her forehead.

It's almost believable; the way she staggers,
the way raspy *oh gods* spurt from her lips.
Today, the glass would have decapitated her,
head bouncing on the pavement like a basketball,
blood geysering from her neck like a Vegas fountain.

But this is 1974 and a mother impaled by glass
is about as much horror as we can stand.
The desensitization will begin in the 80s,
the viscera on the visor generation.
As LA breaks apart, this woman is giving us
30 seconds of raw, pure emotion before she falls
out of frame never to be seen again.

Who were you, lady?
Did anything come before or after?
Did you even get to meet Heston or Gardner?
Did you die on the sidewalk or were you taken
to the makeshift hospital in the car park
only to die in the flood and aftershock?
You should have been the star, the survivor,
the shard a trophy beaming from your exposed skull.

From Her to Eternity

— for Solveig Dommartin

For seven days I wish you undead.
As long as your name doesn't appear
in the news, the only evidence is this:
a three-line note to tell your final hours,
last words, how you left this world.

Here's another beautiful woman dead
in the city of lights, another ghost
to haunt familiar streets, when I cross
Place de la Concord or myself
in St. Sulpice where Jacob wrestles
with the angel or himself. You did both,
until January stilled your heart.

For seven days the silent east
gives me hope, as search engines
yield no results, and I perfect chants,
resist candles, hide matches,
but your face glows in the dark,
head bowed, lips parted, a red siren
swaying to a discordant Nick Cave beat.

Although we are connected by wires
and words fly through the air between
hot boxes, your death comes slowly,
as if you've burned out the circuitry,
refused to be reduced to binary string,
not after those years traveling the earth
in radiant flesh.

Selfishly, I wish I could dance with you
one last time in your waltz around
the globe, until we are both out of breath,
your laughter and curls wild with life.
Swoon. I'll catch you.

Controlled Burn

It's as if the building is on fire,
smoke clinging low to the ground,
a filthy sweet fog rolling in from
the southwest to dirty up the city.

In the barbecue restaurant, all tang
and wood-scented, every eye
is fixed on the news, necks craned,
as anchors with serious voices
express concern, but no answers,
then cut to war in the Middle East
while tongues go back to licking ribs.

Later, it will be explained as a series
of human errors, 3,000 acres burning,
misunderstanding of wind patterns,
and inevitable oversight panels,
so someone can take the blame.

Driving home, sun filters through
the haze, sets every skyscraper on fire,
a preamble to coming night, and the air
smells like past and premonition.

I Was Letty Mason

— The Wind, 1928

At first, I could only tell you in silent, flickering images, title cards, round eyes, fists clenched against my teeth. Now that I have been given a voice, know this: He raped me and stayed the night as sand blew through the cracks. My husband was on the range rounding up the horses, but I didn't love him either. Once upon a time, I would have married Wirt Roddy, been his cattle baron bride, but the night he came to the dust bowl shack, when his fist at the door sounded like the wind knocking, I would have gladly taken my husband's calloused hands, bitten nails and mangled declarations of love. In the morning, I shot Wirt and left him in a drift. Through the window, I watched a sandstorm bury and exhume his body over and over as the wind howled madness into me. Don't believe everything you see. I didn't magically fall in love with my husband and the barren land; I wandered into the desert to die. The Indians believed the North Wind was a great white horse kicking and bucking the sky. When I finally tamed him, the grit filling my lungs and picking my bones clean, I was no longer afraid of anything.

Inglewood

We are lost in this hotel, roaming
hallways, channel surfing, sleep
refuses to come, even after we have.
Sex is easy.

At this height, the windstorm
is a moan and constant crack,
the buildings of downtown
shrouded in dust and smoke
from fires in the hills. We sit
wide awake, silently watching
each other's reflection in the window,
piecing together the lost two years.

We could never love each other.
You were too determined for LA life,
and I can only stomach it for four days,
before the east calls me home.
And I'm too old for you anyway.
You've got a husband who loves you
in West Hollywood and although he's
recently become a stranger,
we are no longer familiars.
We speak different English now,
the flyover states an ocean.

Next morning, you'll go back to Sunset
fast life, waiting for an earthquake to come.
I'll drive through storm debris, running
late for my flight back to my cheap apartment
and dead-end job, writing poems about the wind.

4.
A KISS BEFORE DYING

The Waiting Room

Everyone here is going blind.
The woman in the wheelchair
speaks in gasps as if she's drowning,
while another behind me laughs
under her breath every two minutes
like clockwork, a coquettish little tick.
Across from me, a grizzled black man naps,
his face slack from missing teeth.
And my mother, suddenly old,
her beauty hidden behind sunken eyes,
sharp cheekbones and untamed hair.

When a nurse calls their names,
one by one they all rise unsteadily,
still surprised at the effort it takes.
The doctor will give them all bad news:
glaucoma, cataracts, degeneration.
The slow switching off of lights
until the world is a keyhole, a pinprick.

Alone in the waiting room, I see myself
reflected and distorted in window glass.
I look wide and dim and flat.
When I stand, I feel a twinge in my knee
that makes me pause, swallow hard.
There are more unwanted surprises to come.

The Trial

The television networks know you're dying, maybe alone or with a frazzled caretaker numbed into silence as the afternoon courtroom shows gavel in, punctuated by commercials for lift chairs, walk-in baths, life insurance, medical alert pendants for the inevitable fall. And between those, there is the cancer and the lawyers telling you who to sue for the asbestos, weed killer, or talcum powder that caused your unfortunate affliction.

But what if it's good old-fashioned stomach cancer? That's how the doctor told us in a poor attempt to lighten my mother's diagnosis. Like the networks, he already knew she was dying. The radical treatments on a woman her age killers themselves: removal of vital organs, weeks of intense chemo and radiation, a feeding tube. She makes her own radical choice, which is to do nothing. They tell her what to expect at the end, to scare her into action, but she is resolute.

For two years and one month, you would never guess she had cancer. She convinced herself she did not, that it was malpractice, that maybe she should hire one of those television law firms. Until she wakes up one morning in blinding pain and wants to go to the emergency room. Since she opted for no treatment, so do they. She falls asleep waiting to be discharged, to be sent home to die in front of the TV that never lets you forget the gavel will fall and the decision is final.

Wish

The needle gleams, plunges.
I hold my breath thinking
it will break on her skin
like she's a superhero.
But when it slides in,
she no longer flinches
only makes a sound like a sigh
of resignation and falls asleep.

Like my mother, I wondered
if the doctors were wrong.
I stopped counting the days
since diagnosis, stopped
spending the inheritance,
or imagining life beyond her.

I wished death upon her:
at night before I slept,
after another nasty phone call,
to her face when she was
dressing down a hapless
server for the texture of food.

I try to remember a time
when I put her in the rarified
air of Wonder Woman,
Jaime Sommers or Princess Leia.

I lie awake one night in a chair
by her bed trying to find this
elusive era and never do.
She was always mortal,
quick to anger, often indifferent,
twice adulterous, unforgiving
of slights real and imaginary.

Now I have my wish,
and I'm not certain
I would take it back.

Terminal Agitation

The stacking and unstacking of pillows,
the pinning and unpinning of hair.

The rearranging and invention of words,
the unearthly cries and whispers.

Shouts and tears turn to low moans
then rev up to demonic growls.

Death has many faces, busy hands,
the work of leaving a kind of dismantling.

Maybe it is the sound and movement
of the soul coming unmoored

from its berth, the unsticking
and scraping away of one life for the next.

Renditioned

Although it's only 20 miles
my mother screams she's being
sent away to die, abducted
to a town not her own.
She wants to die at home
in the odd nest of pillows
she built in front of the TV.
Eventually unable to walk
then to even sit up,
the pillows become a fort
that she disassembles
and reassembles
in a desperate attempt to
fortify her position –
against pain, encroaching
death and us – the caretaker
jailers, her would-be executioners.
"I know my rights," she growls.
"I'm not going anywhere."
When the hospice ambulance
arrives, she tries to bargain
with the nurse: she needs
two days to get her affairs
in order then she'll go.
When the nurse shakes her head,
there is outright refusal,
but the papers have been
signed and the nurse gives her a choice:
the easy way or the hard way.
Mother chooses the latter.
Immune to sedation, she grabs
at furniture as the gurney passes,
then at the door frame.

As they restrain her, she claims
torture and kidnapping.
Tells them I am the enemy.
Her final hours, like her life,
will be the hard way.

Hospice

Death has a scent —
almost like rotting meat —
sweet and sour pungent.
It's five days unfed and unwatered,
the throat a chimney.
This was what she feared most:
the withholding of food and water.
Her skin turning to parchment,
tongue swollen with thirst.
If she could speak, she would
never speak to us again.

Strange Angels

The week before my mother died
the house was full of wasps.
They buzzed and bumped along the ceiling,
got caught in the curtains and blinds.
Angry and in search of exit, yet refusing
every open door and window.

After the nurse came
and told my mother she would be dead
in a week, the wasps hovered near her
but never landed or threatened,
and she never swatted them away.

In witchcraft, a wasp is a strong feminine spirt,
a guardian and protector.
The caretaker, a deeply religious woman,
said the devil was in the house, unleashed
prayers and insecticide to down and drown them.
But these wasps were impervious,
resurrecting and wobbling back to the air.

The day after my mother died in hospice,
the husks of the dead wasps littered the carpet,
seemingly fallen mid-flight.
Their manifest, tethered to my mother's rage,
gone out of them along with the sting.

The moon the night before my mother dies

Perfectly low peekaboo
pregnant with light
it looks like a cutout

Photoshop cinematic
greeting card sentimental
a perfect oval yolk

it hangs over the unreality
of this night, false gravity
even as you prepare to float away

Vigil

While my mother's body disappears,
deflates and curls for departure,
I sit next to her and expand.
The 100 pounds I lost cut to 80
as if I'm taking on her weight,
her anger, grief, and fear tipping
into me like an hourglass.
In her delirium, she says
she'd take me with her if she could,
leaving as easy as a one-way bus ticket,
to join my father and the rest of the
lost family. But instead, I'm buoyant
on fast food burgers, forbidden sweets,
no longer solid by sublimated.
So that when the time comes, I'll drift
like an errant beachball on the tide
back to the shore, while my mother
races to the horizon, chasing last light,
and light as a feather.

My mother uploads herself to the World Wide Web

Although she never used a computer, my mother inadvertently uploaded herself to the World Wide Web as she passed out of this world on her way to the next. She was convinced that computers were gateways to trouble and fraud and she'd forgotten how to type anyway. In hospice, as evening falls, she mistakes the glow of my laptop for the last exit, that starry tunnel to heaven. Her eyes open wide, her mouth an O of wonder, as she draws a deep breath followed by a long exhale that fleetingly fogs the screen as she goes. I momentarily feel guilty, after urging her just hours before to go toward the light should it appear. I imagine her angry at this un-expected diversion, but hopeful that her enlightened mind floods with the possibilities. Released from her turncoat body and brain, she travels cyberspace to all the places she never got to visit in the flesh, riding the cloud to her next destination. And the next. And the next. And the next.

Sex In My Parents' House (a sequel)

This time, they won't come home and catch us. They are already downstairs in matching plastic boxes on the fireplace mantle. This lack of interruption, the absence of adrenaline, fear of discovery diminished and scattered like their ashes soon will be. I'm face down on my childhood bed as barely legal pounds his boredom and restlessness into me, trying out dirty talk he heard in a porn clip. I'm a long way from Lee, who is a ghost of a different kind now, the one who got away and never returned. My dismissal of him absolute and unforgivable even after 30 years. The number seizes me up, sends me into a nostalgia spiral. I can fit into my 1989 clothes again, the music is a click away, the films too. But here's what I haven't told you yet as the boy finishes and pulls on his jeans for quick departure: this isn't my house. The house of the baby blue carpet I grew up in was sold long ago. My parents bought this one after I moved out, downsized. It was a place they could afford and never felt like a home even to them. It was just a way station on the road to heart disease and diabetes, blindness, and cancer. Even their ghosts don't linger here. There is no one to see me. The carpet is beige.

Pilot of the Airwaves

Hidden in the back of the vanity, a letter never sent, or maybe returned, tucked inside the paper sleeve of a 45rpm from 40 years ago. A song I hadn't heard or thought about since 1979 when I mistook Charlie Dore for Juice Newton or — sacrilege — Joni Mitchell.

It's the farewell soundtrack to a lover given up the year before in the heat of reconciliation. Blue ink in my mother's delicate cursive: "Remember how much we loved this song? I miss listening to it with you." I imagine my mother and her lover tuned in to AM gold, diddling in the Food Giant parking lot or necking behind Majik Market where they thought no one would see them. Everyone saw. There were anonymous phone calls, warnings in the mailbox, sidelong glances in the hardware store. My father remained stone-faced and stoic for reasons I couldn't fathom.

Until one morning, driving me to school, the CB radio in his Plymouth crackled to life with a honeyed voice. "Plumber Man, you got your ears on? This is Ruby Blue, come back." She was in need of his services, something about a leak he'd fixed before, and the grin that spread across my dad's face was a revelation. They talked in lingo and numbers — 10s, 20s and 88s — I didn't understand, but it sounded flirty and familiar. Before I got out of the car she said, "Hey, this just came on the radio" and a tune punctuated by pops and static filled the car.

Ooooh, you make the nighttime race
Ooooh, I don't need to see your face
You're sounding good...

Sitting on the floor in my dead parents' house this memory is suddenly 5 by 5 — loud and clear — as I use my phone to look up lyrics and trucker slang. On closer inspection, the handwriting isn't my mother's at all. Well, well, Daddy-O... This was a letter received and worthy of secreting away, perhaps the song played when no one was home. This poem is for the girl who didn't sign her name. Whoever, wherever you are, Ruby Blue, thank you for making my dad smile and all those 88s — love and kisses.

Caché

Trap door hinges protest,
dust and spiders fall
along with poison pellets
the mice never ate.

And hidden up there
are the faces of strangers
collected by my uncle
in San Francisco.

Dreamy-eyed boys,
alone and together,
before the great quake
and later Prohibition.

There's irrepressible life
rather than serious stillness,
defying stateliness
in favor of joy. Even then.

They adorned Terry's walls
before the darkness came,
witnessed the plague years
from mute, untouchable past.

A continent away, nameless
but not lost. Now on my wall,
ready to see what comes next,
be it disaster or belle epoque.

My mother returns after 268 days in the bardo

My mother returns unannounced and unexpectedly, the key I'd given her – lost in the tumult of death – rattling the lock. The door opens and she walks in on sturdy, striding legs, her right arm loose and swinging – a sight unseen since 1986 – almost like I remember her, before madness and maladies turned out the lights. In the liminal, she's learned to walk again, discovered muscle memory, regained her vision. She's dressed in garish, day glow yellow shorts with black sandals worn over pantyhose, lips fire engine red. But this is only an echo of a past life: she's fuzzy around the edges, slipping focus, at last becoming unattached. Gone, too, is the anger and despair that lived in her voice for so many years replaced with a smile, a laugh, a palpable unburdened lightness. Now she's off for one last night of bingo, maybe some slots, defying rituals and norms, as is her custom. After that, she hasn't the least idea where she's going and finds it very pleasant not to know. This is the mother meditation she will leave with me, along with the key on the counter which means she will never be here again.

The Clarity of Loss

This year I did not mark
the day of your death.
I let it slip by in an afternoon
filled with music you'll never hear,
words you'll never read,
a chorus of voices raised in protest
at the unwavering passage of time.
I don't need a number
to know that you are gone.

Since you went away, other tragedies
have left their toll, the media
mining the fragile, the exhaustion,
the relentless sorrow of things we cannot change.
We have made high art out of twisted cars,
planes crashing, buildings falling, bullets in the dark.

I have dissected my past into little pieces
and put them in their proper places.
I have begun the process of growing up
and older, of stripping down memories
to their essence and casting off the extraneous.

Even without a calendar, we will be born
and die, clockwork beyond our control.
And there is a clarity in loss
because it reveals the true path, the one common
experience, the thing we all share.
You have died and I will join you, and time,
which we have enslaved ourselves to, will snap,
and in whatever an instant is,
it will be as if we never parted.

Why my grandmother lives in a lantern

Because she didn't want a boring urn or to be scattered to the wind or buried like a campfire. Because I was trusted with her beloved son's remains and he resides in a fashionable vase befitting his impeccable taste. Where do you put a woman who lived so many lives? Who survived religious fanatic parents, a drunken abusive husband, an impossible daughter, illnesses that should have killed her long before cancer at 89. Who cleaned houses, motel rooms, hospital bedpans, washed others' clothes to make ends meet. Who loved to go honky-tonking, drive cross-country, take up with younger men, answered to the nickname Moom Moom. Who after the diagnosis pragmatically planned her own funeral to the letter except this one thing. Who said leave me in the plastic crematorium box until you find the *right place*. And it sat for days on my coffee table, a monolith, as I awaited a message. Then I stubbed my toe on the iron lantern that had been sitting next to my door for two decades, always empty and in search of purpose, without light. I turned the lantern on its side and opened its hinged door, sat the bag of ash and bone atop the dark opening. After a moment, the bag quivered then slipped inside like sand passing through the neck of an hourglass. Home at last and decidedly un-boring. Sometimes, when the evening light is just right and dances across the floor, it catches the lantern just so and Moom Moom glows inside. Because as vessels go, I can think of nothing more appropriate than being a guardian against darkness.

Flamenco Sketches (Demo)

~Four-bar vamp~

Saturday pandemic drive
grey and improvised
over empty interstate lanes.

Miles fades in and out
signal stretched
across low clouds, near mist.

Momentary lockdown lift
this piece has no melody, just modes
a gist of Spain in the linger.

Drift wist, sun blown buzzing
a standing wave all brass
wasted on pavement.

Improvise a solo outing, like this:
flame etches or men catches
oceans alone or these chests.

Let's try it again, take six
not a demo, not this
pandem(ic)(onium).

The lump

appears behind my ear
seemingly overnight
mouth stroke droops
and I diagnose tumor
even before the doctor

tells me it's stage four
rare and recurrent
silently metastasizing
to the brain and lungs
my future fate sealed

by poor diet or
sucking strange dick or
final mother curse but
still a surprise and
an inevitability

Post-op art

Three days before I see my face again.
The left side dripping like a Dali
off the bruised tree limb of my cheek.
My Van Gogh ear cut off and reattached.
And surely Mary Shelley must have
had some future sight of me for her monster,
the jagged scar running ear to ear across
my throat, the drains like Frankenstein bolts.
Or maybe Jayne through the windshield.
Either way, I've been decapitated
and sewn back together.
Under ether for eight hours, head hollowed
out like a jack-o-lantern with a lopsided grin.

Radiation mask

Someone said it feels like a day at the spa.
I say it feels like conscious mummification,
breathing in warm and wet as it grows cold
and hard around my head.
The next time I see it, lying on a table,
my own face stares back at me from
a plasticized death shroud.
And, as I'm locked to the table,
something akin to being buried alive,
even the brightest pop music diversion
sounds funereal.

Hit me with those laser beams

Fire those proton torpedoes
directly at my head.
Burn me from the inside out.
You don't see it or hear it,
but there's a smell
that permeates the mask
that has you headlocked
to the table that twists away and up
into a space odyssey
not of your choosing.
Maybe it's the smell
of the high burst over Hiroshima,
the ozone layer breakdown,
years of my life melting away.
And when it's done, my neck
glows toxic red and the honeycomb
imprinted on my face takes
hours to fade, irradiated bees
buzzing in my cheek.

The let go

Things I never thought I'd part with while alive
shoved into outstretched hands, pitched into dumpsters,
left for others to deal with disposal.
These books I'll never read again, films I'll never watch,
heirlooms that will wind up with strangers or buried
in a landfill must be given up. The coffin or oven
won't be big enough to take it all with me.
For a moment, I feel cleansed and unburdened
but my new rooms feel curiously incomplete.
Mourning the ephemera of my life.

Divisadero

It will take days but what else is there,
at least this seems like something done,
little pinches of your ashes from coat pocket
up and down Divisadero to the Castro.
Doorways, drains, patches of grass, blowing you
like a kiss in the wind, fairy dust or a spell being cast,
to put you back where you belong, everywhere
in this city where you once came alive.
Up into the tangle of electric bus lines,
clinging to the marquee lights, swept
out into the morning light of the closing bars
and bathhouses.
Sylvester's falsetto in my ear on repeat,
but I keep changing the words to *mighty surreal*.
Because what else is there to say about the dead
walking the dead back home?

Ev'ry time we say goodbye

— with Peter, Krys & Dave at St. Clement's Church

The church door slams behind me
with a ferocity only God could muster.
Now he's got me inside 12th-century walls
with the dead under my feet and history
swirling in the rafters. I am nothing,
a speck of dust passing through, a pilgrim
visiting the heretic in the cemetery.
Derek is out there, his slate black headstone
a monolith, no date of birth or death,
only the engraved flourish of his own signature.
Nothing else is necessary.

I saw you before I knew your work,
flickering in childhood home movies
on Annie Lennox's face
as she lamented you with Cole Porter.
You were supposed to direct the music video,
but were too ill, so instead, you became the star.
I was at a party and it was background music
while Damien begged me for sex
despite his diagnosis, condoms spilling
from his pockets like gold coins.
Fuck me while I'm still pretty, he begged.

And then Annie and that song again,
serenading Edward II and Gaveston
as they part, while Christopher
holds my hand in the dark.
Uncle Terry and his lover Jeff beside us,
already knowing their fate, tucked into
each other, becoming shadows
of their former selves, singing quietly:
Ev'ry time we say goodbye
I die a little...

Kneeling in the Old Romney churchyard
ten thousand days in between,
I hum the song and trace your name,
Derek, make you touchstone and totem
to everyone I've lost.

EXIT MUSIC

Wonderland (AIDS Suite)

To all the cowards and voyeurs, there are no more tickets to the funeral.
— *Diamanda Galás*

1.
A photograph: Terry in a white t-shirt, faded jeans, a copy of *Playboy* in his lap circa 1977 as sunlight rainbows through the window of his San Francisco apartment. It's the Castro, where every day is a party and rubbers were for sissies at the Fairoaks. Who was he trying to fool with that girly mag? Maybe he just liked to read the articles, or maybe it was Iggy Pop's big cock, waving from the stage of a Stooges' concert. I had that same issue, purloined from my dad's stash, pages wrinkled from cum shots, but not on those pristine girls, who enjoyed backgammon, horseback riding and had perfectly shaved pussies.

2.
Terry wrote letters in blue ink on snowy white stationary, and my mother cried over them in the post office parking lot. I was never privy, couldn't find her hiding place. I have a picture of Terry and my mother: in the woods, young, arms draped around each other's shoulders. He came out to her first, softened the blow for my confession. She handled it like a pro, but those letters... what did he say in those letters that made tears rain on the fur collar of that long gray coat she wore? She lost them, doesn't remember, wouldn't say if she did. I could see fire dancing in her eyes.

3.
A litany: Bulldog, Handball, Jaguar, Glory Holes. Terry knew Harvey Milk, saw him the day before he was assassinated, agreed to disagree over the baths, which Harvey had sworn off and Terry frequented. In 1978, Harvey gunned down in city hall, followed by riot, vigil and silence. Supervisor soothsayer predicted bullets to his brain. Could he see what else was coming? The season of marches and death upon them all, the bathhouses clouded with "gay cancer," the first acronym, GRID, transmuted to a word that once meant care, but became letters for extinction. AIDS.

4.

While Ronnie-Rayguns exchanged arms for hostages and the Red
Cross sat on its dirty needles, Terry fell out a window trying to break
into his locked apartment. Down he went, six stories, a service shaft,
his fall slowed by pipes and wires he ripped through like a hot knife.
The doctors gave him pint after pint of freshly squeezed blood, cold
and untested, along with the standard issue "miracle he survived."
All the bruises would eventually fade save one. The KS calling card, a
kiss of death, on his lower torso. The how and why ceased to matter
in a spiral of red tape. Persecution, crucifixion, homicide, genocide.

5.

A vague memory: Terry packing to leave, escaping the long, slow
death of being gay in the South, heading west to Oz. When he
decided it was safe to return, he moved into the same apartment
in Atlanta he'd abandoned a decade before. Made it love nest. I lost
track of all the boyfriends, until Jeff finally stuck. The bad news
came in a long distance call, a last cackle from the Wicked Witch,
who installed herself as mayor and wielded a deadly wand over a
once Emerald City. Terry and Jeff, holding hands, promising to go
down together. Pills stockpiled in medicine cabinet and bedside ta-
ble never used. Jeff would go first, quick and unplanned, the disease
exercising its right to take you fast or let you linger in agony. I was on
the phone with Terry as they took Jeff's body out of the apartment.
He would be banned from the funeral.

6.

The day before he died — withered in a hospital bed, slipping in and
out of delirium, Jeff gone a year — Terry heard voices, saw shadows
moving, lamented he'd never go dancing again. I promised to bring
him the tape of a disco song he'd heard on the radio, but never got
the chance. I have it on my shelf, dusty and un-played. He left while
I sat in grid-locked traffic after a frantic summons. That night, I
kept another promise and swept his apartment clean of porn, bags
full of fuzzy and fading '70s and '80s movies, where cum dripped
unchecked from every orifice, not a condom in sight. He forgot the
nudie photos, later found by my grandmother, an angel bare-assed
in chaps haloed by unearthly light.

7.

At the memorial, everyone speaking in contained voices, I let mine
crack with tears, opened the door for my mother and grandmother
to sob, got dirty looks from his friends for bringing down an oth-
erwise lighthearted remembrance. Before Terry, I'd always had
the stiff-upper lip inherited from English genes, now I cry easily at
death, even strangers, and Terry's gone 10 years and AIDS is pan-
demic, still not a cure in sight. I still have the picture of Terry in his
San Francisco apartment, the one he dreamed about as he drove
cross-country, leaving Atlanta. Next stop wonderland.

ACKNOWLEDGMENTS

Some of the poems in this new & selected that did not appear in previous collections were originally published in these journals.

Animal: The Beat of Black Wings

Assaracus: I Was Letty Mason

Blue Fifth Review: New Car Smell; From Her to Eternity

Chantarelle's Notebook: Strange Angels; Terminal Agitation

Divining Divas Anthology: Meeting Jeanne Moreau

Ekphrastic Review: The Last Confession of Sister Ruth

Georgia Center for the Book: Saving Anne Sexton

Hobble Creek Review: The Waiting Room

Impossible Archetype: At Prospect Cottage; Five Days in LA

In Posse Review: Spring Hill

Kentucky Review: The woman with glass in her face

Limp Wrist: Roosters & Hens

LOCUSPOINT: Controlled Burn; LA poetry reading; Inglewood

MiPoesias: Crave

New Delta Review: As the rush comes

Ouroboros Review: Velocity

The Pedestal: Wonderland (AIDS Suite)

SubtleTea: Credentials

VerseWright: At Lake Forest Plaza; Xenomorphs

The title of this collection was suggested by Laure-Anne Bosselaar's poem "Ocean Rooms" from her collection *These Many Rooms* (2019, Four Way Books) and given her kind blessing.

To these fine poets and friends who have inspired and supported me along the way: Karen Head, Cecilia Woloch, Julie E. Bloemeke, Donna Kile, Megan Volpert, Cherryl Floyd-Miller, Steven Reigns, Kathy Dean, Agnes Meadows, Vanessa Daou, Lisa Allender, Tania Rochelle, Bryan Borland, Seth Pennington, Tanya Keyser, Kate Evans, Franklin Abbott, Kodak Harrison, Theresa Davis, Dan Veach, Colin Potts, Tina Miller, Malory Mibab, Joy Thompson, TJ Geer, Jacob Nguyen, Christeen Snell, Jennifer and Denton Perry, Ivy Alvarez, John Carder Bush, Charles Guan, Anderson Rodriguez, Ken Cloudt, Peter Kotowski and the late Jackie Sheeler.

Thanks to the publishers of the collections and chapbooks many of these poems originally appeared in: Poetry Atlanta Press, Metro-Mania Press, Seven Kitchens Press, Finishing Line Press, and Sibling Rivalry Press.

Many thanks to Elizabeth Holmes, who has designed the majority of my book covers over the years, including this one. The photos on the cover are of my uncle, Terry Graves, in his apartments in San Francisco and Atlanta in the 1970s and '80s, and also a photo of him with his partner, Jeff.

ABOUT THE AUTHOR

Collin Kelley is the author of the poetry collections *Midnight in a Perfect World* (Sibling Rivalry Press), *Better To Travel* (Poetry Atlanta Press), *Slow To Burn* (Seven Kitchens Press), and *Render* (Sibling Rivalry Press), chosen by the American Library Association for its 2014 Over the Rainbow Book List. He is also the author of The Venus Trilogy of novels — *Conquering Venus*, *Remain In Light*, and *Leaving Paris* — also published by Sibling Rivalry Press. *Remain In Light* was the runner-up for the 2013 Georgia Author of the Year Award in Fiction and a 2012 finalist for the Townsend Prize for Fiction. Kelley is also the author of the short story collection, *Kiss Shot* (Amazon Kindle Exclusive). A recipient of the Georgia Author of the Year Award and Deep South Writers Award, Kelley's poetry, reviews, essays, and interviews have appeared in magazines, journals and anthologies around the world. With Karen Head he co-edited *Mother Mary Comes To Me: A Pop Culture Poetry Anthology* (Madville Publishing), which was named a 2022 Book All Georgians Should Read by Georgia Center for the Book.

www.ingramcontent.com/pod-product-compliance
Lightning Source LLC
Chambersburg PA
CBHW020415130626
46549CB00006B/2568